Lila and Andy learn about Recycling

Kenneth Adams

Book Cover by Kenneth Adams
Illustrations by Kenneth Adams
First Edition 2025

ISBN: 978-1-998552-10-8

When in doubt, find out!

Hi there! I'm Lila, and this is my brother, Andy! Today, we are spending time exploring a recycling center in our town. The huge machines, colorful bins, and busy workers make this a magical place.

We decided to visit a recycling center when we noticed the amount of things our family throws away every single day. Waste like empty milk cartons, cans, cardboard boxes and plastic containers quickly fills our garbage bins. But what happens to all the stuff we no longer want? We know we have to put different items in different colored bins, but where do they go after that?

From the moment we decide to recycle something, it goes on an incredible journey where old stuff is changed into something brand new.

Come on! Let's explore the recycling world together!

Understanding the Recycling Symbol

Before we learn how recycling works, let's talk about that famous recycling symbol we see everywhere. It consists of three arrows forming a triangle! Each arrow represents an important part of the recycling process.

Reduce: Reduce means to cut back on or lower the amount of trash we make.

Reuse: Reuse means to find other ways to use things instead of throwing them away.

Recycle: Recycling is the process through which old things are turned into new products.

PET

HDPE

PVC

LDPE

PP

PS

OTHER

Know Your Numbers

When you look at plastic containers, you'll see a number between 1 and 7 inside the recycling symbol.

Here's what they mean:

#1 (PET): Plastic bottles and food containers.

#2 (HDPE): Milk jugs and detergent bottles.

#3 (PVC): Pipes and window frames.

#4 (LDPE): Squeeze bottles and shopping bags.

#5 (PP): Yogurt containers and bottle caps.

#6 (PS): Disposable cutlery and foam packaging.

#7 (Other): Mixed plastics.

Read the glossary at the end of the book to see what the acronyms between the brackets mean. An acronym is a shortened version of a name typically made up of the first letter of each word.

All labels are removed and the plastic bottles are washed.

The plastic bottles are broken down into chunks of plastic.

The plastic is melted at very high temperatures.

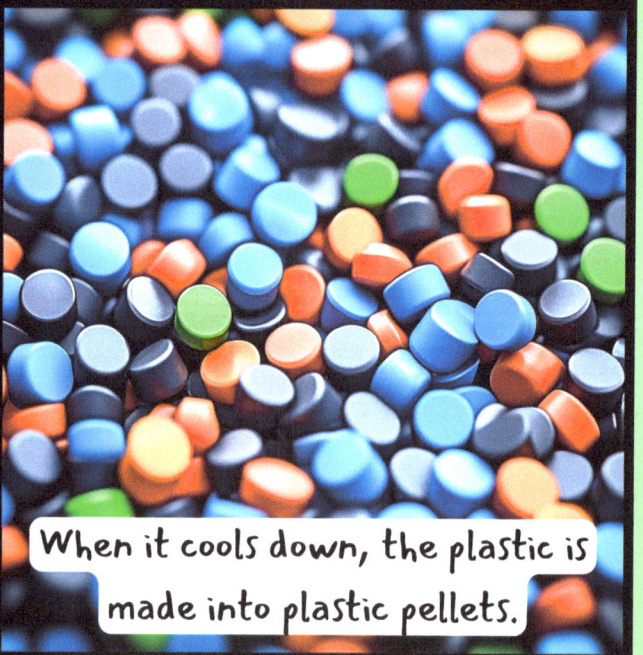

When it cools down, the plastic is made into plastic pellets.

The Recycling Process

What is recycling? Recycling is a process where things we use daily are changed into something else once we don't need them anymore and want to throw them away.

Take a plastic bottle, for example. Its adventure begins with a thorough cleaning to remove any labels or food residue. Then, the bottle is shredded into tiny pieces called "flakes". These flakes are melted down at high temperatures and transformed into small pellets.

Pellets are very small pieces of plastic that can be used to create countless new products, like warm fleece jackets, playground equipment, or even new food containers.

Paper is sorted to keep different types of paper together.

The paper is shredded into smaller pieces.

The shredded pieces of paper are mixed with water to create pulp.

The pulp is pressed into thin layers and dried for reuse.

Paper follows an equally fascinating path. When paper is thrown away, it is carefully sorted before being shredded into small pieces. These pieces are mixed with water to create a pulp, which is then cleaned to remove inks and other contaminants. The clean pulp is pressed, dried, and processed into brand new paper products. Some types of paper can be recycled five to seven times before their fibers become too weak to use again.

<u>Did you know</u> that recycling one ton of paper could save 17 trees and 7,000 gallons, or 26,500 liters, of water?

Metal is crushed or broken down into smaller pieces.

The metal is melted down at very high temperatures.

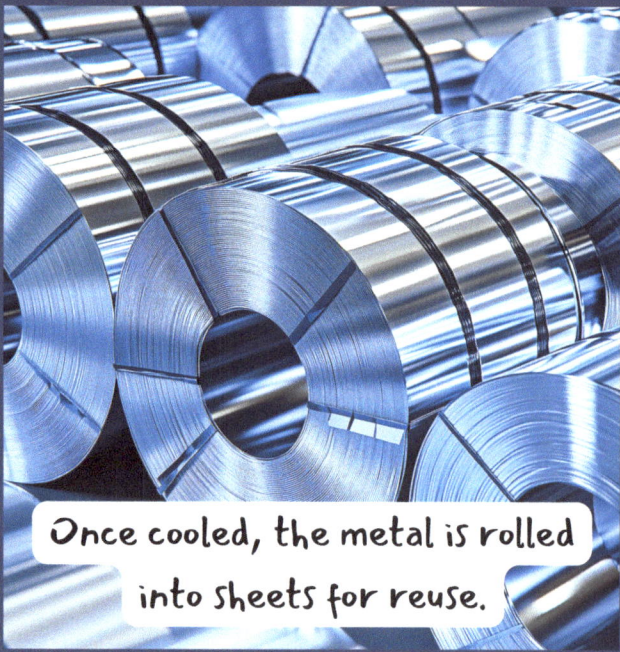
Once cooled, the metal is rolled into sheets for reuse.

The reprocessed metal is used to make new products.

Metal recycling is super easy! Metal, like aluminium and steel, is crushed or broken down, melted at very high temperatures, and then shaped and rolled into metal sheets that can be used to make new metal products.

Steel and aluminium can be melted and reshaped over and over again. Aluminium can go from a can to being recycled and back on the shelf in just 60 days.

<u>Did you know</u> that recycling one aluminium can save enough energy to power a TV for up to three hours?

Glass bottles and jars are cleaned and labels are removed.

The glass is broken down into small pieces called cullet.

The cullet is melted down at very high temperatures.

The melted cullet is reshaped into new glass products.

Glass is also a super sustainable material because it too can be recycled forever without losing any of its quality.

Glass bottles and jars are sorted by their color, cleaned, and smashed into tiny pieces. These tiny pieces of glass are called cullet.

The cullet is melted down at very high temperatures, and then shaped into new glass stuff like bottles and jars.

<u>Did you know</u> one recycled glass bottle saves enough energy to power a computer for almost 30 minutes?

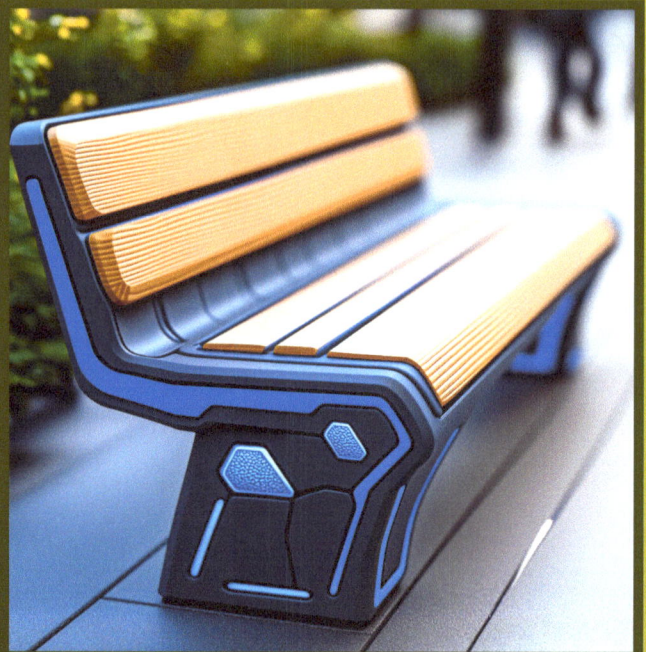

Here are some examples of the cool things your recycled items can be changed into.

- Plastic bottles can be turned into T-shirts, park benches, or new bottles.
- Glass jars can be used in materials to build roads, or become decorative tiles.

- Aluminium cans can become bicycle frames, car parts, or new cans.
- Paper can be used to make egg cartons, paper towels, or notebooks.
- Steel cans are melted down, and can then be used to create construction materials, train tracks, or even appliances like washing machines or refrigerators.

A Global Mission

Why is it so important to reduce the amount of waste we create?

Some studies estimate that the average person produces about 4.4 pounds, or 2.2 kilograms, of trash every day. There is simply not enough space on Earth for us to place all the stuff we don't want or don't need anymore.

And think of all the pollution we create when we dump our waste in landfills or in nature. It affects animal and plant life, and often ends up in streams and rivers, from where it finds its way into our oceans.

Recycling in Sweden is serious business

Germany recycles more than half of all their municipal waste

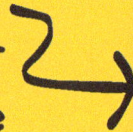

Recycling should also not be limited to only a few countries. The whole world has to work together to keep our planet clean. In many countries, recycling has become a way of life for its citizens, with everyone playing a part in collecting and sorting waste for reuse.

Countries like Germany are already recycling half of all the municipal waste they produce, while others, like Sweden, have become so efficient at recycling that they've run out of enough of their trash and now import garbage from other countries to continue their recycling efforts!

Japan has created a system where they recycle almost all of their metals, and Singapore has transformed its waste into a man-made island called Semakau.

Waste recycling can cause pollution of its own.

Specialized waste recycling processes can be expensive.

The Recycling Challenge

Recycling is a good solution to reduce waste, but it has its challenges. It is an expensive process, and many countries do not have the money to develop the necessary infrastructure to run comprehensive recycling programs.

The recycling process itself requires energy and can sometimes produce emissions, which also cause pollution, and some materials are not so easy to recycle. For instance, certain types of plastics are difficult to process, and may require complicated technologies and specialized equipment that cost a lot.

Materials that become too contaminated often cannot be recycled at all, which means they end up in landfills after all, despite our best intentions.

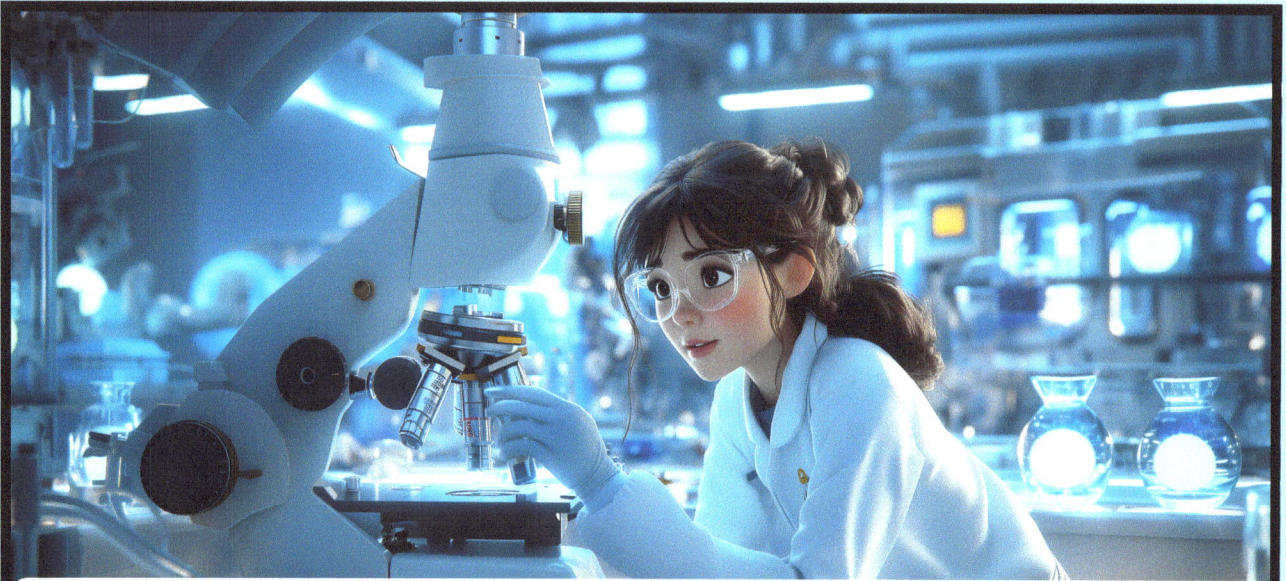
Scientists are continuously developing new ways to recycle.

A modern waste sorting facility.

But there is hope for the future!

Recycling is still a fairly new concept, and scientists and inventors are constantly developing new technologies to make recycling easier and more efficient.

They're working on innovative solutions that could transform how we think about waste, creating methods to reuse materials that were previously considered too difficult to recycle.

AI-powered waste sorting machines.

Plastic-eating bacteria.

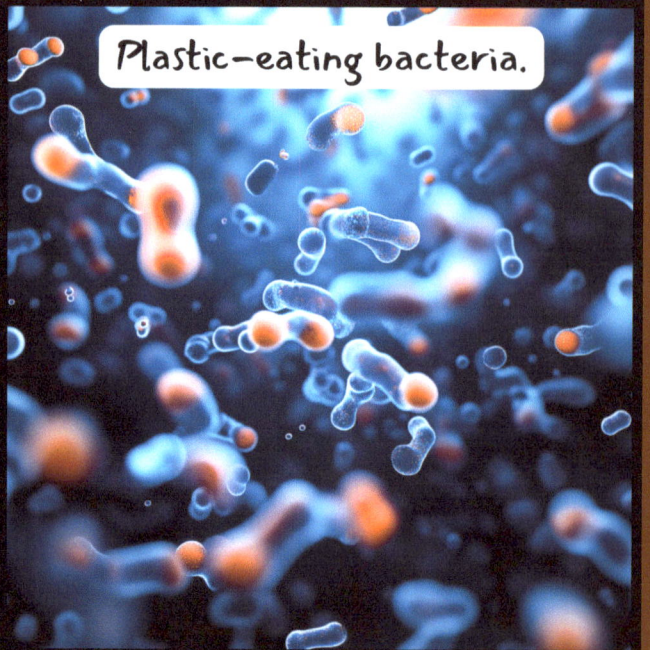

A sustainable recycling facility with solar panels on the roof.

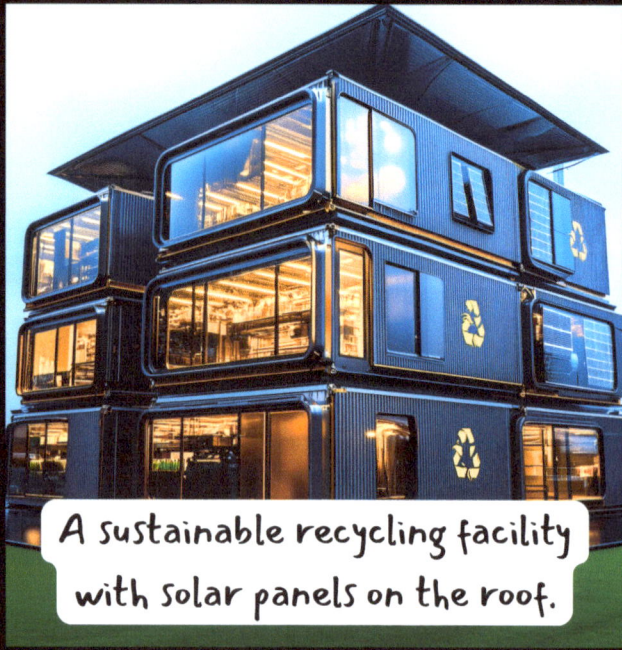

Smart packaging materials.

Here are some examples of the innovations scientists are working on to make recycling easier.

- Self-sorting bins are smart waste bins that sort waste using artificial intelligence (AI). This makes the sorting process so much faster.
- Scientists are studying bacteria that can break down plastic. They hope to find some super plastic-eating bacteria that can help plastic decompose way faster.
- Chemical recycling breaks down plastics into their chemical components. New plastic products can then be made without lowering the material quality.
- Recycling machines that use solar power are great for the environment because they don't need regular electricity.
- Smart packaging materials are specifically designed to be more compatible with existing recycling systems. They contain labels or tech built into them that help people throw them away correctly.

Rinse plastic food containers before recycling them.

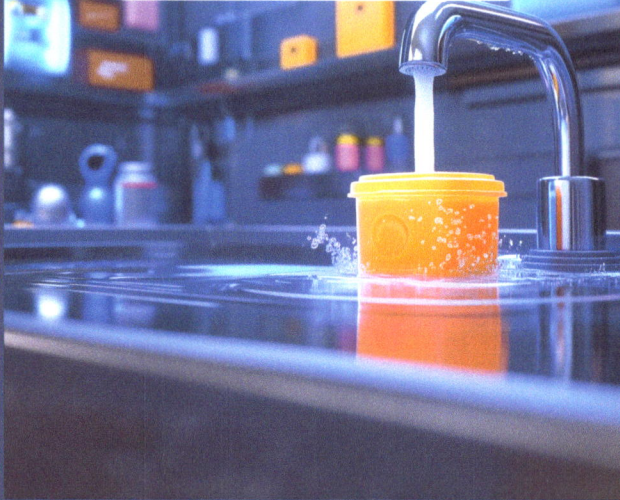

Choose recyclable drink containers.

Use reusable shopping bags.

Becoming a Recycling Champion

Recycling takes much effort to do. It requires you to commit to making better choices with the waste you produce. Learning which items can be recycled in your local community is the first step you can take.

Before placing items in the recycling bin, take a moment to rinse out containers and remove food scraps and labels that could contaminate the recycling process.

When you buy bottled water or soda, choose the ones using recyclable water bottles or cans, and when Mom or Dad goes grocery shopping, encourage them to use reusable shopping bags.

Being a true champion for recycling goes beyond just what you do to reduce waste. It's about inspiring your family and friends to also reduce and recycle waste.

By teaching friends and family about proper recycling techniques, you can inspire others to care about the environment too. Learning about recycling turns everybody into a protector of our only planet.

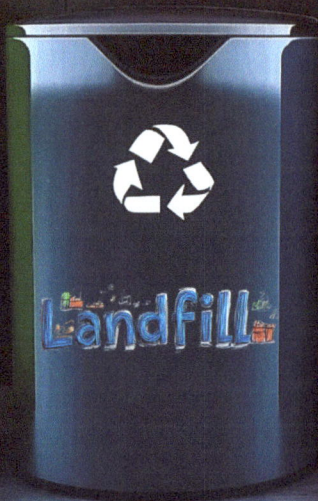

You too can create a successful recycling center at home.

Follow these easy steps:

1. Choose a convenient location.
2. Set up separate bins for different materials.
3. Label bins clearly with pictures and words.
4. Keep a "cheat sheet" nearby for quick reference, so you always know what goes where.
5. Rinse and dry containers before recycling.

Our Recycling Journey

Wow, can you believe how much we've learned about recycling? It's incredible! From a simple plastic bottle or piece of paper to a completely new object, recycling is a magical process of change.

Remember when we used to just throw things in the trash without thinking? Now we know about sorting centers, recycling technologies, and how every single item we recycle can make a big difference! The next time you're about to throw something away, take a moment to think about its potential for a new life.

Join us in making our world cleaner and greener! Every small action counts, and together we can make a huge difference. Start your recycling journey today, and don't forget to share what you learn with others!

Remember, the Earth is our only home, and it's up to us to keep it clean and healthy for future generations.

Goodbye for now, explorers. Continue to ask interesting questions. It's the only way we learn about the world around us!

Glossary of Recycling Terms

A glossary is like a mini-dictionary of terms with definitions for those terms. Here's a glossary of terms used in <u>recycling</u>.

- <u>Aluminium (Aluminum)</u>: A lightweight metal that can be recycled over and over.
- <u>Baling</u>: Squishing recyclables into large blocks for easier transport.
- <u>Bin</u>: A container for collecting recyclables.
- <u>Biodegradable</u>: Materials that can naturally break down into harmless substances over time.
- <u>Carbon Footprint</u>: The amount of carbon dioxide created by our actions.
- <u>Compostable</u>: Things that can break down into natural materials that help plants grow.
- <u>Conservation</u>: Protecting and saving resources.
- <u>Contamination</u>: When non-recyclable items mix with recyclables, making them harder or impossible to recycle.
- <u>Cullet</u>: Crushed glass ready for recycling.
- <u>Curbside Collection</u>: When recycling is picked up from your home.
- <u>Disposal</u>: The way we get rid of things we no longer need or want.
- <u>Drop-off Center</u>: A place where you can take recyclables.
- <u>E-waste</u>: Old electronic items like phones, computers, and tablets that need special recycling.

- <u>Ferrous Metals:</u> Metals that contain iron and can be picked up by magnets.
- <u>Grinding:</u> Breaking materials into small pieces.
- <u>HDPE:</u> High-density polyethylene, a strong plastic used for milk jugs.
- <u>Landfill:</u> A special area where trash is buried in the ground.
- <u>LDPE:</u> Low-density polyethylene, a flexible plastic used for bags.
- <u>Marine Debris:</u> Trash that ends up in oceans and waterways.
- <u>Materials Recovery:</u> The process of getting useful materials from waste.
- <u>PET/PETE:</u> Polyethylene terephthalate, used for drink bottles.
- <u>PP:</u> Polypropylene, used for bottle caps and food containers.
- <u>PS:</u> Polystyrene, also known as Styrofoam.
- <u>Pulping:</u> Turning paper into a soft, wet mixture for recycling.
- <u>PVC:</u> Polyvinyl chloride, used for pipes and some packaging.
- <u>Raw Materials:</u> Natural resources used to make new products.
- <u>Recyclable:</u> Items that can be processed and made into new products.
- <u>Shredding:</u> Cutting materials into smaller pieces.
- <u>Sorting:</u> Separating different types of recyclables.
- <u>Sustainability:</u> Using resources in a way that won't harm future generations.
- <u>Transfer Station:</u> A building where waste is collected before going to its final destination.
- <u>Waste Management:</u> The collection, transport, and disposal of waste.
- <u>Zero Waste:</u> A goal of sending nothing to landfills.

Here's a short quiz to see how much you learned from this book:

Multiple Choice

1. How many times can a sheet of paper typically be recycled before its fibers become too weak?
    a) 2-3 times
    b) 5-7 times
    c) 10-12 times
    d) Indefinitely

2. Which country imports garbage from other nations because they're so efficient at recycling?
    a) Norway
    b) Finland
    c) Sweden
    d) Denmark

3. What number is typically found on plastic milk jugs?
    a) #1
    b) #2
    c) #3
    d) #4

4. How many pounds of trash does the average person produce daily?
   a) 2.2 pounds
   b) 3.3 pounds
   c) 4.4 pounds
   d) 5.5 pounds

5. How long does it take for an aluminum can to go from recycling bin back to the store shelf?
   a) 30 days
   b) 45 days
   c) 60 days
   d) 90 days

<u>True or False</u>

6. Glass can be recycled indefinitely without losing its quality.

7. All types of plastic can be recycled in your home recycling bin.

8. Plastic bags can go in the same recycling bin as plastic bottles.

9. Food-contaminated containers can still be recycled without cleaning them.

10. Metal objects need to be completely rust-free to be recycled.

Fill in the Blank

11. The three R's of recycling stand for _____, _____, and _____.

12. A _____ is a special area where trash is buried in the ground.

13. _____ is the term for converting materials into lower-quality products.

14. The process of turning paper into a soft, wet mixture for recycling is called _____.

Short Answer

15. Name three items that can be made from recycled plastic bottles.

16. Why can't you put plastic bags in regular recycling bins?

17. Name two things that should be done before recycling food containers.

18. How does recycling one aluminum can help save energy? Be specific!

Answers

Multiple Choice
1. b) 5-7 times
2. c) Sweden
3. b) #2
4. c) 4.4 pounds
5. c) 60 days

True or False
6. True
7. False (many types require special recycling)
8. False (plastic bags require special recycling)
9. False (containers must be clean)
10. False (rust is acceptable on metal items)

Fill in the Blank
11. Reduce, Reuse, Recycle
12. Landfill
13. Downcycling
14. Pulping

Short Answer
15. Acceptable answers include: T-shirts, fleece jackets, park benches, new bottles, playground equipment, carpeting

16. They can tangle in machinery and halt the recycling process, requiring special handling at specific facilities

17. Acceptable answers (need two):
    - Rinse out containers
    - Remove food residue
    - Remove labels (if required)
    - Remove caps (if different material)

18. Recycling one aluminum can saves enough energy to power a television for three hours

Take a look at the other subjects Lila and Andy are learning about...

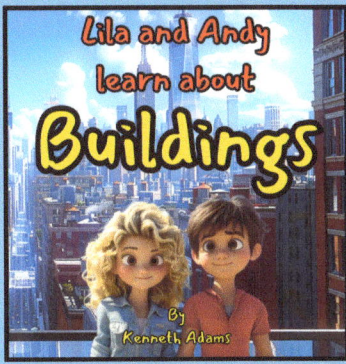

Lila and Andy learn about **Buildings**
By Kenneth Adams

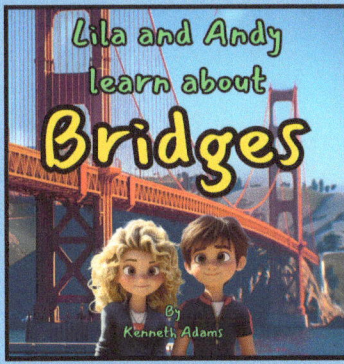

Lila and Andy learn about **Bridges**
By Kenneth Adams

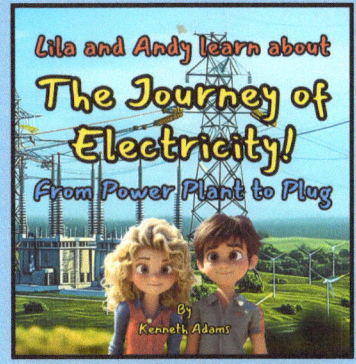

Lila and Andy learn about **The Journey of Electricity!**
From Power Plant to Plug
By Kenneth Adams

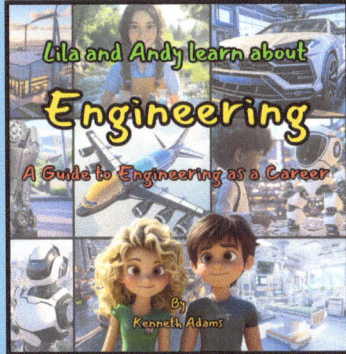

Lila and Andy learn about **Engineering**
A Guide to Engineering as a Career
By Kenneth Adams

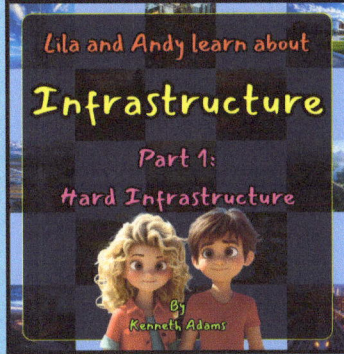

Lila and Andy learn about **Infrastructure**
Part 1:
Hard Infrastructure
By Kenneth Adams

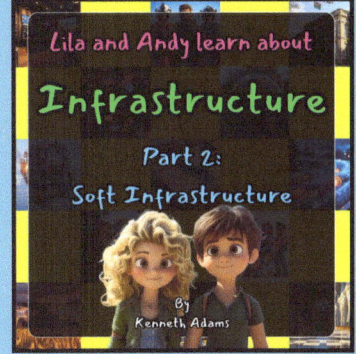

Lila and Andy learn about **Infrastructure**
Part 2:
Soft Infrastructure
By Kenneth Adams

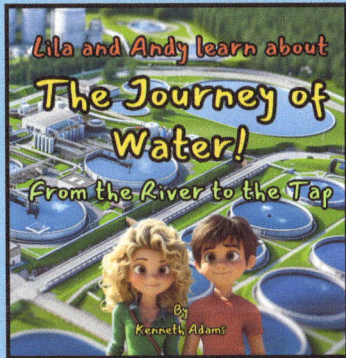

Lila and Andy learn about **The Journey of Water!**
From the River to the Tap
By Kenneth Adams

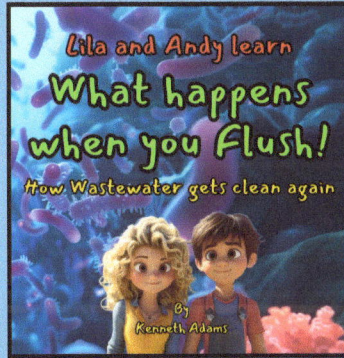

Lila and Andy learn **What happens when you Flush!**
How Wastewater gets clean again
By Kenneth Adams

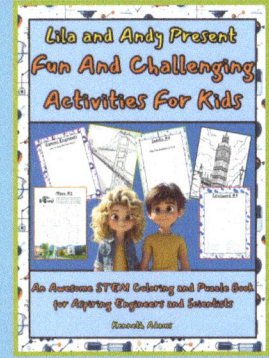

Lila and Andy Present **Fun And Challenging Activities For Kids**
An Awesome STEM Coloring and Puzzle Book for Aspiring Engineers and Scientists
Kenneth Adams

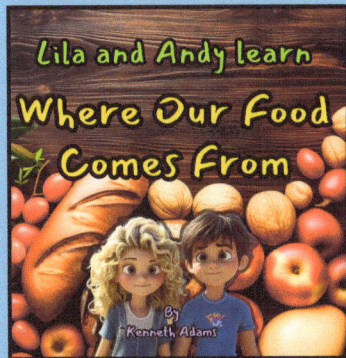

Lila and Andy learn **Where Our Food Comes From**
By Kenneth Adams

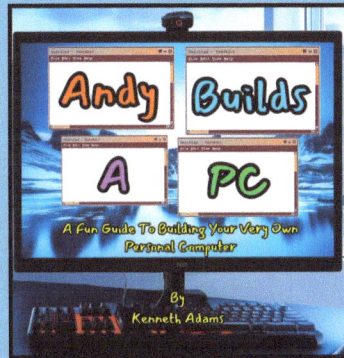

Andy Builds A PC
A Fun Guide To Building Your Very Own Personal Computer
By Kenneth Adams

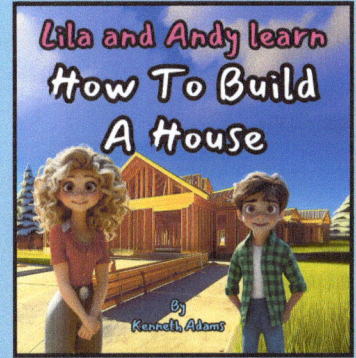

Lila and Andy learn **How To Build A House**
By Kenneth Adams

www.ingramcontent.com/pod-product-compliance
Lightning Source LLC
LaVergne TN
LVHW072134070426
835513LV00003B/102